About the Author

Elijah Rice is a self-taught writer, from Maine, born in January of 1996. He has spent most of his life working in kitchens desperately wanting to be creative for a living. He grew up quite poor so most of his influence comes from books and movies from the library, PBS, and his good old Nintendo 64.

Illustrated by
Marianne Cavanagh Yost

The Incredibly Strange Thoughts of Life

Elijah Rice

The Incredibly Strange Thoughts of Life

PEGASUS PAPERBACK

© Copyright 2025
Elijah Rice

The right of Elijah Rice to be identified as author of this work
has been asserted by him in accordance with the Copyright,
Designs and Patents Act 1988

All Rights Reserved

No reproduction, copy or transmission of this publication
may be made without written permission.
No paragraph of this publication may be reproduced,
copied or transmitted save with the written permission of the publisher,
or in accordance with the provisions
of the Copyright Act 1956 (as amended).

This is a work of fiction. Names, characters, businesses, places, events
and incidents are either the products of the author's imagination or
used in a fictitious manner. Any resemblance to actual persons, living or
dead, or actual events is purely coincidental.

Any person who does any unauthorized act in relation to this publication
may be liable to criminal prosecution and civil claims for damage.

A CIP catalogue record for this title is available from the British Library

ISBN-978-1-80468-080-3

Pegasus is an imprint of
Pegasus Elliot MacKenzie Publishers Ltd.
www.pegasuspublishers.com

First Published in 2025

Pegasus
Sheraton House Castle Park
Cambridge CB3 0AX England

Thoughts You Have First Thing in the Morning

Oh God, not this again.

I'm just forcing myself to be up, but I could definitely keep sleeping.

They say, "Breakfast is the most important meal of the day." Personally, I think that's just marketing... although, it is my favorite.

I woke up this morning,
the sun was shining,
the sky was clear and blue,
with birds chirping a lovely morning tune.
Perfect kind of day to shut the curtains
and play video games all day long.

Time to get out of bed… gotta start the day.
Come on… let's get going.
Or…
I could just lie here for another hour and pretend like
I don't have to pee…
Yeah, I'll do that.

I've always said I'm a morning person, but I don't know if I say that because I really am a morning person, or if it's because I'm cursed to wake up at 5:30 a.m. no matter what time I go to bed.

Why is it that when I'm trying to fall asleep, the bed is the most unnatural, uncomfortable,
hardest place in the world, and I feel like I'm trying to sleep on the side of the road?
But when I wake up, it's like I'm being enveloped by an angel, and not a fiber of my being wants to leave?

I'm just forcing myself to get up now.

BUT!

I could *definitely* keep sleeping.

Coffee Thoughts

Sip
"Man, this coffee is delicious."

Sip
"You know what would make this better?"

Sip
"A nice warm pastry, fresh out of the oven"

Sip
"Mmmm, I should go get one"

Sip
"Aaaaand the coffee is gone."

"…Better get more coffee to drink while I think about which pastry to get."

Even bad coffee smells like good coffee.

Mmmm, I do enjoy some good coffee, but if I don't drink it black, will coffee snobs look down on me? Do I need to pretend I only drink black coffee just to get people off my back, when in reality, I would down a Starbie's caramel macchiato in a heartbeat?

I do like black coffee, I also like expensive coffee, I even enjoy fresh ground, but I keep these thoughts to myself because I don't want to look like a coffee snob.

I think the only people more insufferable than coffee snobs are people who actively hate coffee.

Is coffee a drug?
Am I addicted to it?
Or do people who say that feel the need to project their own insecurities onto me because of their own shortcomings?

I don't understand why pretending to like these people needs to be a part of this job.

Sometimes, I wonder why I continue to show up to work on time when everyone else shows up ten to fifteen minutes late…guess I'm the A-hole for making everyone else look bad.

They say everybody's working for the weekend, but I'm usually working on the weekend.

If one more tiny thing slightly inconveniences me,
I think I'm just gonna walk out.

I only have five more hours, that means I only need twenty more fifteen-minute periods.

I work as hard as I can, to get the most amount of work done as soon as I can; that way I can go home and be lazy that much faster.

> Gotta love answering to people
> that aren't as qualified as I am.

Oh, I take five extra minutes on my break and it's a big deal, but Bill, who is routinely thirty minutes late from break, gets a pass.

Sometimes, I hope my boss says or does something horrible and offensive to me, just so I can file a lawsuit against him, and hopefully, never work again. That's right, Jerry, keep making me do things that are against the law because you're ignorant and didn't bother learning employment laws before starting a business.
It's only a matter of time.

I wonder if anyone would notice if I… just left for a little while.

Sometimes I think adults are more childish than children. Then I go to work, and everyone confirms my suspicions

I agreed to cover a shift for a coworker. I'll be glad to have the extra money, but boy, at the moment, do I hate myself for saying yes.

That's definitely not correct, but I'm just going to pretend that I don't know it.

No, go ahead and take your every hour on the hour, five-minute smoke break. I'll be here, working, not taking a break.

They say if you work hard, you'll go far in life.

But I have found that if you work hard,

they want to keep you right where you are,

because if they promote you,

they'll have to find someone else to do your job.

But you're already the best at it...

I think this game is rigged.

One day, when I'm a millionaire, I'm going to buy this place and close it down for the good of humanity.

Interpreting My Own Dreams

I have a lot of dreams where I'm on a bridge and it begins to collapse, or I'm driving down a bridge and the bridge is under construction, so I end up driving off and falling to my death. Now, you might think this means I have a fear of heights, but I think what's actually haunting my dreams is the fear of America's crumbling infrastructure.

I once had a dream where I was a superhero, ya know, doing all the "alien from another planet crash landing in the Midwest" type things. Yet, I couldn't keep my eyes open. I was so tired in my dream that it kept me from saving those around me. My eyes clearly represent me, and my eyelids represent the pressures of society. So, while I have the ability to help myself and others, society will always keep me down. Or it could mean I'm not getting enough sleep.

The other night, I had a dream that a river suddenly appeared outside of my house, flooding the whole town and causing a great deal of damage. I had to use a power cable to rescue people floating down the stream before they were crushed by the dam at the end of the river, which had only just appeared moments before. This can only be about a sudden onset of IBS. The river suddenly appearing without warning, causing a great panic. The power cord, not plugged in, represents the powerless feeling of an unrecoverable public disaster. Trying to save the people before it's too late shows the urgency with which you must act, because time is running out to reach a safe place to deal with IBS. So, my brain must have been warning me to never eat frozen chimichangas before bed again.

Last night, I had a dream that I was driving home and a waiter was chasing after me. No matter how fast I drove, he continued to run faster, keeping pace with my car. Suddenly, I slammed on my brakes to try and make him run into my car, but just as I was about to hit him, he vanished. I turned back to the front window, and there he was, standing on my hood, smiling. Then, he smashed his hand through the windshield and asked me if I needed any change. The waiter clearly represents my past failings always coming back to get me. No matter how long it's been, my past actions will have an impact on my life-- hence, the change. I'm sure this has nothing to do with the fact that I forgot to tip the waiter at the restaurant last night.

I have a lot of dreams where I'm naked, but I think I'm not going to interpret those ones and just keep them to myself.

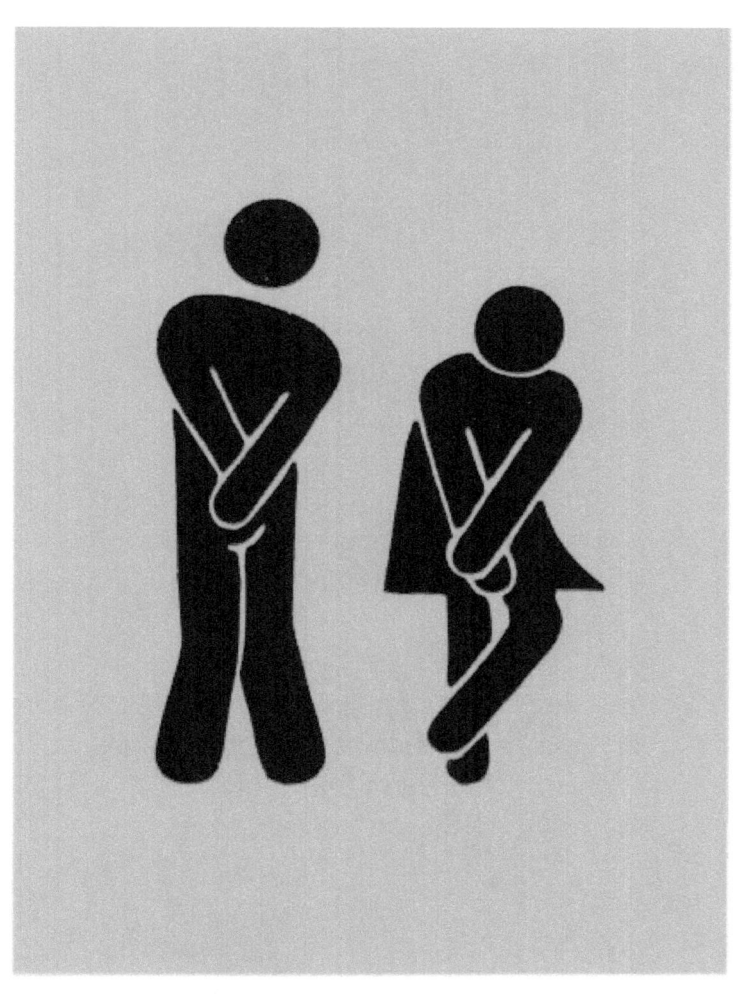

Thoughts While Using a Public Restroom

I'm going to pretend like I don't see
that rather large brown stain.

I'm not sure if porta potties are considered public
restrooms or not. I don't really have a greater
thought on this topic;
I'm just not sure.

It's amazing how much people stop caring once they start using a public restroom. It's like they're playing a game, and the goal is to cover as much of the floor, walls, and ceiling as possible.

All public restrooms smell, but not all public restrooms smell the same, which is a little concerning since the same thing happens in all public restrooms.

I once went on a two-week vacation with a friend who refused to use public restrooms the whole time, even in the hotel. I'm pretty sure he ended up buying new pants once we got back.

I'm not sure a two-foot gap between the wall of the stall and the floor is necessary. While I'm at it, I'm not sure the gap in the door, large enough for a whole pancake to slide through, is necessary either.

Thoughts While Dating

I think this person is cool. I'm not quite sure what to do from here…
Guess I just go up and talk to them, right?
No. That can't be it.

At what point does it stop being dating, and start being permanently attached un-legally?

This is nothing like the simulations.

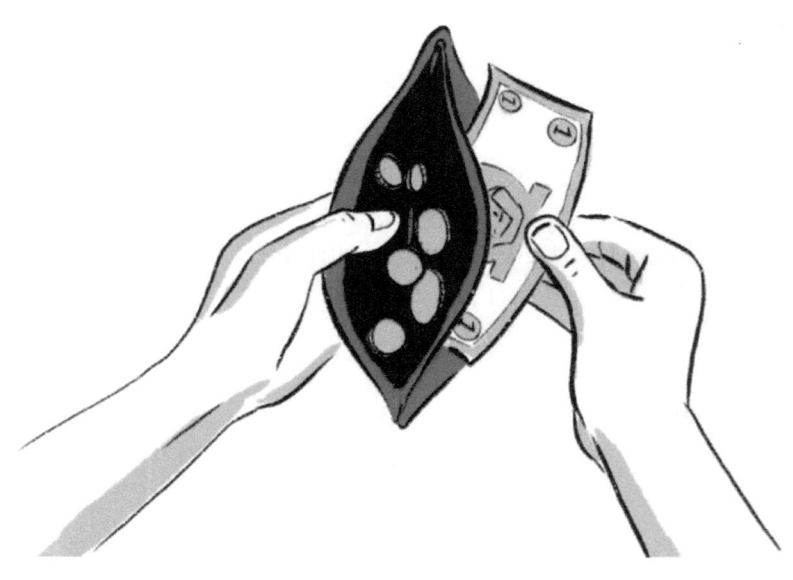

What's the best date out there for $1.76?

I hear there are rules to dating, but nobody ever gave me the rule book. It seems like one side is playing with an unfair advantage. The only one I know is, "Do not pass GO, do not collect $200."

I like smart women, but I gotta ask myself: am I even smart enough for a smart woman? I feel like if I have to ask, the answer is no…

I'll never date a rocket surgeon.
There are so many dating apps out there these days.
I remember back in the day, when you'd pick up
women in MMORPGs.

Coffee is always a safe bet for a first date, but there are exceptions.
Local hipster spot = Good
Washington's Finest Star = Okay
DD = Bad
McD = Perfect

A date is really just a job interview at the end of the day.

Dating is like a box of chocolates. As in, I brought a box of chocolates for my date, and she didn't even give me one... which sucks... like life...
I'm confusing metaphors, but you get it.

There should be an eject button for bad dates. Like, you press it and the wait staff runs over, lifts up your chair with great gusto, and tosses you out of the restaurant as a tiny parachute comes out of the chair, leaving the other party to pay.

Marriage and All the Things You Think About

My wife says I need to eat better because she wants me around for a long time. What the hell does she know? Clearly not much since she thinks under salting my food is a good idea.
For "health reasons".

I think my wife looks just as good after a long day of work as she does when doing herself up right before a date.

I'm pretty sure ungodly snoring is grounds for divorce.

I'm pretty sure my wife is about to ask me to do a favor. I better ask her to do the same favor first.

Sometimes you offer solutions, sometimes you're just an ear to be vented to. Never, ever get these two situations mixed up.

Have I told her this before?

Just because you're married, doesn't mean you have to stop dating each other.

Before getting married,
I never saw myself caring about curtains.

If neither of you remember exactly what was said and who was exactly right, be sure to double down and tell them you're right. Some may call this gaslighting, but it's not like they know either. So, who's gaslighting who?

I wonder, in a house fire, who my wife would pull out first: me, or the pets?

Thoughts While You Do the Sex

Trying something new really could be the highway to the danger zone.

Do I go with the beat or the rhythm?

I should really be able to count this as my daily exercise.

Sixty seconds is both longer and shorter than you might think.

I can feel the people in the posters on my wall judging me. They're just jealous because they're 2D images and I'm not.

I think the cats just broke something downstairs, but I'm just going to ignore that for the time being.

I really need to tighten up the bolts on the bed frame.

Now this is podracing!

Things are going well, but I have a cramp in my leg.
If I change my position, it will be better, but there's
just no way to do that smoothly.

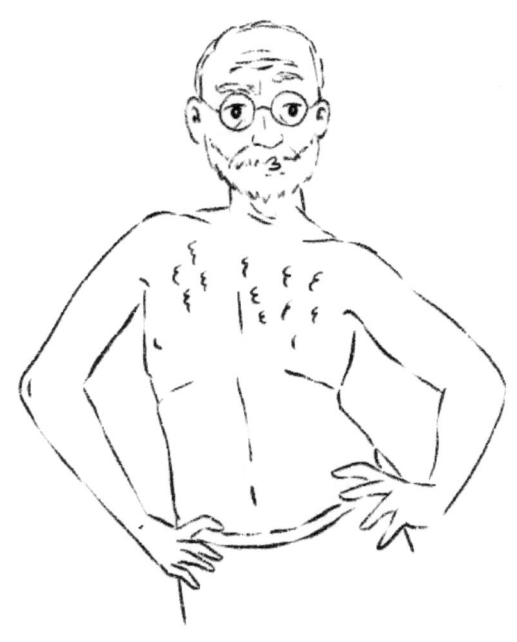

Why are random family members popping into
my head? Ugh,
paging Doctor Freud… Oh God,
now I'm just thinking about Sigmund Freud!

Thoughts While Cooking.

Recipe, shmecipe… wait, what do I do again?

If this sauce separates one more time, I'm going to throw the pan as hard as I can against the wall.

Why can I never cook rice?!
Too much water, mush.
Too little water, scorched.
The perfect amount of water, I still get it wrong.

Pssh, I know how to microwave something, I don't need to keep the box… wait, how long is this supposed to go for? Ugh, looks like I'm digging through the trash.

People say turkey is bad and always dry.
I say
most people don't know how to cook turkey.

Some people don't cook fish, because they believe it will make their house smell of fish forever. These people are morons.

Salt, pepper, garlic powder, and onion powder.
That's 90% of all the seasonings you will ever need.

There are enough spices in my cupboard for 17th-century England to invade my house.

I either make enough food to feed one person, or
enough to feed a small army.
There is no in-between.

Doing the dishes while cooking is far and away the
best method of doing the dishes, Especially since,
after I cook and eat, I'm probably not moving for at
least an hour, and in an hour, I am not going to be in
a state to do dishes.

I know the best way to cook is low and slow,
but I only have the patience for huge and fast.

I walked away for two minutes, and everything has gone wrong!

It's not too late to order out.

Thoughts You Have While Waiting for Food to Arrive.

This truly is the longest forty-five minutes
has ever felt.

I hope I live long enough
for instant food teleportation.

I sense it approaching...
nope...
just hunger delusions.

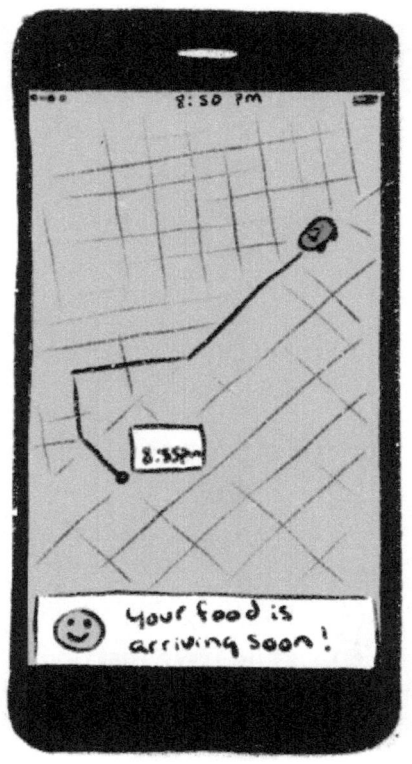

Watching the little car on the app is a fun way to pass the time.

If the driver eats my food, I'll simply eat the
driver.

Running late, and I'm starving:
maybe I should have just cooked?
Nah.

When the food gets here, I can't answer the door too fast. Gotta hang back a few seconds so it doesn't look like I've been watching and waiting like a pirate in the crow's nest, desperately searching for land. Wouldn't want him to think I'm weird or anything.

Terrible Campaign Slogans

RICE 2032
Let's Do This Thing!

RICE 2032
You? Me? This Tuesday?

RICE 2032

It Could Always Be Worse.

RICE 2032

Why Not?

RICE 2032

We Haven't Even Begun to
See Rock Bottom!

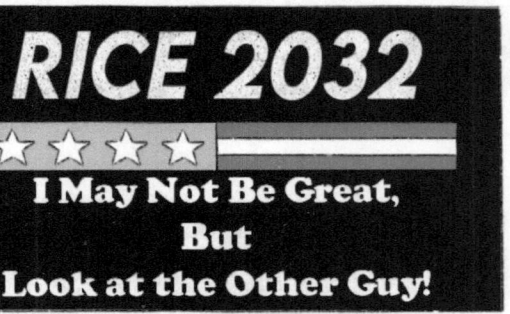

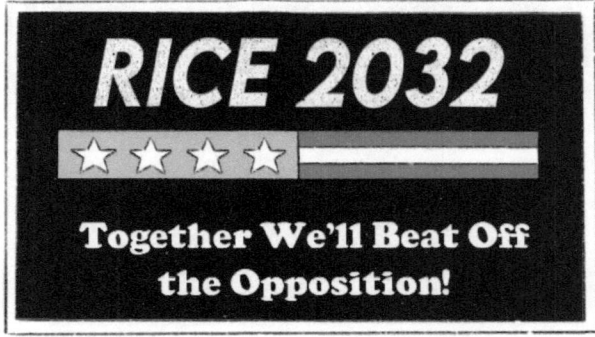

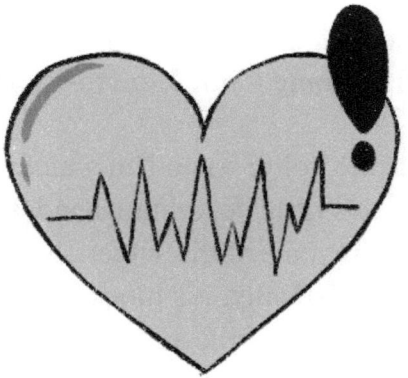

Things That Really Get Me Going, But Probably Shouldn't

You know what really gets me going? Sinks where the faucet isn't centered with the drain. We're dealing with some serious plumbing here. You may take it for granted, but sinks are an incredible invention that make life so much better. That being said, why can't we take a hot minute and make sure things are centered and symmetrical? It looks sloppy, and when I want to rinse something out, it feels better to be right over the drain and see the water go down with no fuss than to watch it slosh all over the sink like some kind of micro-tsunami.

It really gets me going when I'm watching TV and one of my wife's little decorations and doodads slip and block a tiny part of the screen. Now, I have a 55-in TV, so realistically, it's blocking 1/1000 of the screen, but it literally kills any and all enjoyment I get out of my local TV programming. Now, I have to get up and move the thing, but if it weren't there, I'd just be sitting and being lazy in front of the TV. If I'm watching the local Public Broadcasting Service, I don't want to get up. So basically, my day is ruined. At least ruined for the thirty seconds it takes for me to get up and fix the problem.

One thing that really grinds the knot in my feathers is backtracking. I don't mean just walking into another room and realizing you've forgotten something, so you need to go back—though that is also annoying. I mean any kind of backtracking. If I can't move forward, it really puts me in a mood. If I'm taking a hike, and I were to come upon two paths, a shorter one and a longer one, but the shorter one requires doubling back, I'll take the longer one ten times out of ten.

Now, maybe I could examine this information and think, "Wow, that's not reasonable or very rational. Maybe I should go see a mental health professional to see if all of my other so-called quirks add up to something." I shan't, though. I shall continue to live in annoyance.

Why, for the love of God, can my body not decide if it's hot or cold at night? One second, I'm lying in bed, all cozy and snuggled up, and bam! My body is like, "Bro, what are you doing? You are literally on fire! You are going to die if you don't do something. SEND IN THE GALLONS OF SWEAT!" So, I stick my leg out to get relief, and it feels good. I'm nice and relaxed again, only for my body to kick me in the gut with, "DUDE! WHAT ARE YOU DOING? Don't you know it's a blizzard out here? You are going to get frostbite and your leg will fall off! Send in the chills all the way up the spine!" And I'm just laying here like, "What do you want from me?"

If you are online and you see a post that you agree with but have nothing to add to the conversation, stop commenting "This." Just don't. I'm sorry you can't think of anything deep or clever to say, but you still want to signal to people that this is the side of the line you stand on. I'm sorry that just hitting like isn't enough for you. Saying "this" is just as bad as the people who say "Louder for the people in the back." You look like a fool who isn't capable of an original thought. It makes me uncomfortable- Not because your solidarity makes me feel uncomfortable, but because you're giving me secondhand embarrassment, and being embarrassed makes me feel very uncomfortable.

Thinking About Gaming

I don't know how to admit to my friends that I'm just not that into tabletop RPGs.

The older I get, the less fun I have playing games online. I dunno, maybe I just don't like nine-year-olds hurling slurs at me.

I know you didn't use full strength on that spinner.

If I turn my head and controller, it'll make my kart turn better. Them's just the facts.

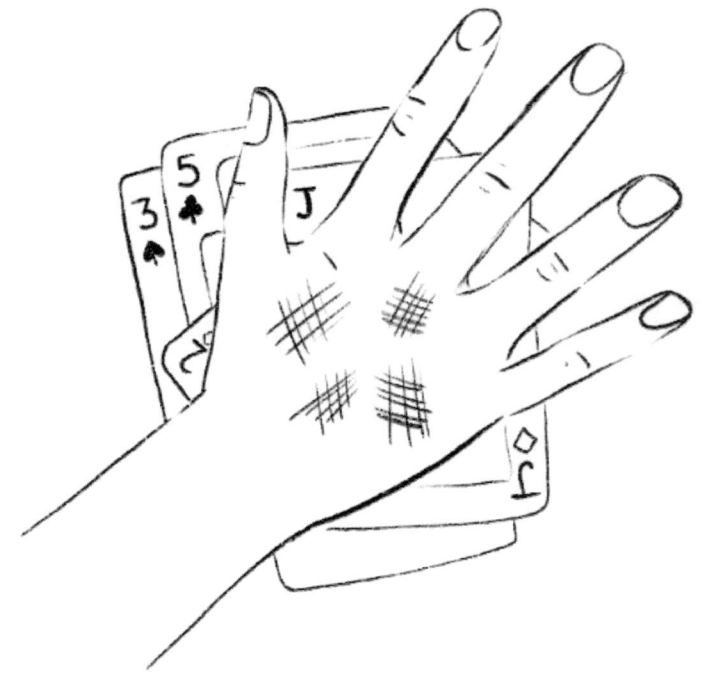

Is it even Slap Jack if you don't try to bruise your friend's hand?

I got work tomorrow,
so I'll only play for a little bit...
damn, it's three a.m.

Why are you taking so long to make a move? What do you mean you aren't thinking about your turn and live-updating it in your head while everyone else takes their turn? This is why everyone thinks board games take so long.

I don't care if we're married. All bets are off when playing Italian Plumber Party.

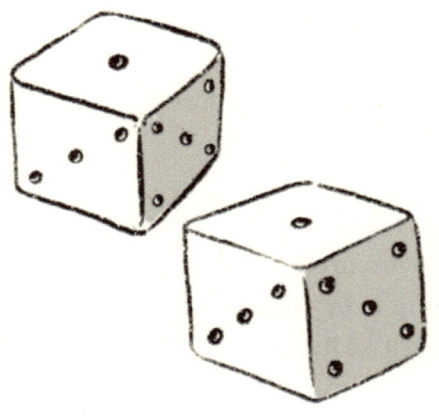

Another low roll?

No way these aren't loaded!

Dudes really be out here showing me a clip of a kill they got in 2007.

I'll win on my next turn so long as no one screws me over on their turn… and I've been screwed immediately.

Ping 1295? Yeah, I'll still try it.

After spending thousands of dollars on a high-end PC, and paying top dollar for the best internet, I have come to the conclusion that it wasn't actually lag… it was me.

I don't currently have the mental dexterity to walk
all the way across the map right now.
So, I'll probably just stop playing for the day.
I mean come on,
that would take like ten minutes IRL.

If my little brother keeps talking smack, I'm going
to stop going easy on him and kill all his enjoyment
of this game. I will make him cry!

Hey, look, it's a summer sale. Perfect time to save
some money and drop $329 on games I may or may
not ever play.

Better than all my friends, not good enough to play online. Such is the curse of a slightly above mid-tier gamer.

I love it when I've been playing a game for six hours only to realize I put all my skill points in all the wrong places and built a completely useless character. So realistically, I need to restart the whole game.

Bro, if aliens came to Earth, promising to not to destroy the planet if we beat them in a game of Italian Plumber Kart, I am the one to do it.

Oh, my friend is over to play some games, better pull out the third-party controller held together by strategically placed tape.

Sport Thought

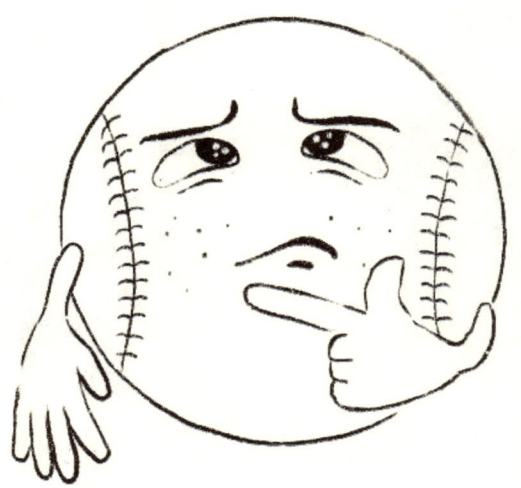

I could probably do that.

God, I hate
(insert name of player who is on another team, who is objectively better than anyone on your team, but can't publicly admit here).

You drink to celebrate your team's success and you drink to be consoled in your team's defeat.

OOOO, that was a big hit, I hope he's okay. I mean he is an opponent, but I don't want him to be actually hurt. Although, I'd be lying to myself if I don't acknowledge the fact that his absence would be good for my guys. I don't think that makes me a bad person... Does it?

Yes…yes….Yes…YESSS…YES….WHY?!

I have to use the restroom, so I'll wait until the commercial break. But then, something happens right before the commercial that makes the commercial break too intense to relieve myself. So, I usually just end up holding it for four hours.

I literally hate every single person in (insert city where your team's rival plays).

Why don't they just do the same thing I do in the video game version?

I really love it when the game is half over, and I can tell that my team has just given up. Yes, the other team put up forty-seven points in the first half, but that means it's technically possible for us to do the same.

I require nothing less than total domination.

I AM FILLED WITH DUDE-BRO ENERGY!

Shower Thoughts

I can tell the hot water is getting low, but I really don't want to get out.
I have two options:

Option A – Get out now and having enjoyed a nice hot, though quicker than I wanted, shower.
Option B – Stay until the water gets cold and say that I had a terrible shower because the heat ran out, even though it was perfect for 98% of the shower.

It's always option B.

Last time I was in the shower, I noticed I used the rest of the shampoo, does that mean I've replaced it for this shower... no.

It's not entirely impossible that I won't slip, crack my head open, and die in this shower. At least the water would wash out all my dirty thoughts.

If I look down, will I see my feet?
I think this is a test best left to the hypothetical.

I hate it when people try to tell me
I should take cold showers

"FoR tHe HeALtH beNeFItS"

All you're really trying to do is convince me
that you're better than me.

Thoughts While Grocery Shopping

Oh, chicken is on sale.

If I buy this breast, I could make some great chicken sandwiches… but, if I buy it, I'll have to walk all the way back to produce to get lettuce, and then I'll need to walk all the way to the baked goods, which is on the opposite side of the store. Is my desire for sandwiches worth the extra walking?

Ten items or less people, it's really not that hard. I mean, this guy clearly has like thirty things in his cart. I mean, I have like fifteen things, but at least they're all small.

The longer I'm in here, the more of my soul gets sucked out of me.

Oh shoot, I forgot to make a list. Oh well, I'll just wing it, that always goes well.

Oh goddamnit,

they changed the whole store again… for some reason.

Ooooohh, peaches are on sale this week!

Don't mind if I do.

The fact that I actively enjoy grocery shopping is a sign that my youth is over.

One time, I bought one red pepper, and one mushroom, and it came out to $10. That's when I knew this "life" thing was a scam.

Okay, are they out of beans, or am I just blind? I better stare at the exact same spot for a little longer, just to be safe.

I know I paid for all these items; I know I haven't stolen anything. But what if the alarm goes off anyway, and I accidentally stole a TV or something?

Turns out, I had mayo at the house.

When I was a kid, I loved playing video games,
I had all the time in the world to play them. But
I had no money to buy them.
Now, I'm an adult, and have money to buy all the
games I could ever want,
but no time to play them.

I need a real adult, 'cause I'm definitely not it, and if
I am, boy, are we all screwed.

I wonder if anyone noticed when I mispronounced
"inavitibly," God, I hope not.

Fifteen years ago, I had an extremely awkward encounter with a cashier when I thought I had enough money, but I didn't.
I really wish I hadn't done that.

I think a lot about how I'll die.
I just hope to God it isn't on the toilet.

I always tell myself if I could go back with all my knowledge, I would be able to change my life for the better, become rich and famous. But I'd probably just make the same mistakes all over again.

One time, I came home from an eighteen-hour day at work, sat on the kitchen floor and cried. Thinking about it makes me feel emotionally worn out all over again.
At least I only have twelve more days until my next day off.

I've never made anyone else cry
as hard as I've made myself cry.

Thoughts of Boredom

You ever want to listen to music, but don't know what kind of mood you're in so you spend the whole time skipping all the songs?

Don't know what to do with myself, so I'm gonna go stare out of each window for a few minutes.

It's nine a.m. on a Monday and all my friends are at work. Why is this my day off?

How do you play the spoons?

I've never noticed until this exact moment, the trim in the room is uneven.

Maybe a nap will cure my boredom… except I'm too bored to nap.

Does drinking cure boredom?
Maybe I should find out…

Bored in the living room.
Now I'm bored in the kitchen.
Oh, maybe I'll go be bored outside.

I kinda wanna play some video games, but I'm not sure what I want to play. I better just scroll through my entire game library for forty-five minutes and then decide to not play anything at all.

After the bombs go off, fighting all my friends and neighbors for what little supplies are left will be a really emotionally devastating situation, except when it comes to Jerry-screw you, Jerry.

If the world ends soon, I'll be able to think of everything I accomplished, which hasn't been much, 'cause my life will be cut short.

Irradiated water is fine, and the fizzy numbing in your mouth is a fun little bonus.

This radiation sickness isn't that bad.

As the raiders begin cutting off my limbs for their feast, I'll pause, smile, and think to myself, "Wow, I won't have to get up for work tomorrow."

At the very least, I'll never have to go to an awkward Thanksgiving again, 'cause most of my family will be dead. But I'll still be thankful.

Grocery stores sure were convenient, but it's super easy to go into your neighbor's house, hold them at gunpoint, and take all their stuff. Less mileage, too.

Can't tell if the Mexican place is still open
Or
if that's just the mound of burning bodies.

We're seven months into the world ending, and my boss still wants to know if I'm coming into work. Like, no, I'm not commuting through fifteen military checkpoints.

Texting Thoughts

I have to send this text real quick, I hope this doesn't lead to a long text exchange, or worse, prompt a phone call.

Sometimes, I worry about sending emojis to people because I don't want to get made fun of for using the wrong emoji. I guess that's how you know I'm getting old.

I'm still not sure about the proper etiquette on who's supposed to send the last text in a conversation.

You ever mean to text someone back and then whoops, it's been three years?

I'mma send this sexy text to my wife… I'm not sure she knew I was flirting… I'mma do it again…

If you ever feel the need to send multiple one-sentence texts instead of just summing it up in one, don't. Just don't do it. I won't be your friend anymore if you do.

I hope it was clear that I was joking because if it isn't, I'mma look like a real D-bag.

I'm gonna open the preview without actually opening the text, this way they won't see I've read it and can't be pressured into responding right away.

Thoughts When You Come Down With The Sickness

Can't tell if this is a cold, the flu or just allergies.

I need to be closer to the bathroom… just in case…
But…
if I move, I think I'm going to need the bathroom right away.

If that bird makes one more sound, open season is about to begin.

I'm feeling a little better today, good enough to go do something, but whenever I do that, I end up getting sicker the next day.
I'm so bored, though!

Why do I have a sore throat all of a sudden?

This is probably it. I should have written a will.
I should tell my mom I love her.

Guess it's time to watch "The Price is Right"
on the couch.

I am too weak, must dig deep,
remote almost in reach!

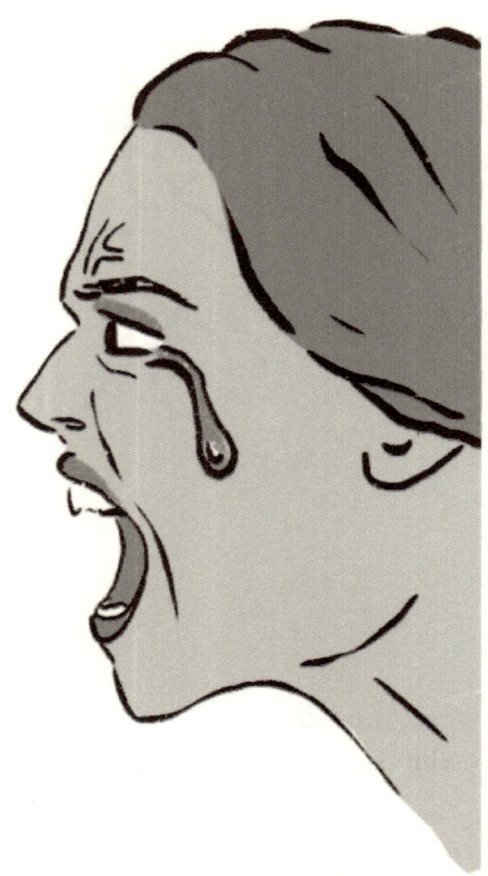

Thoughts When You're in Pain

I can't even move; I'm in so much pain, but I really have to pee. Now the question becomes: should I pee and relieve myself, and just deal with the temporary pain? Or do I lay here and be extra uncomfortable because I'm in pain and have to pee?

The answer is laying here for an hour and then just getting up. Even though I know I'm going to get up anyway, if I ignore it, maybe it'll just go away, even though I know that's not how the human body works.

Oh wow, I didn't even feel myself getting cut, but now that I'm aware of it, it's the most pain I've ever been in.

Can't tell if it's gone away or it's been happening so long that my brain is no longer interested in broadcasting it.

Some people say a broken heart is the worst pain a person can experience. Sounds like a load of BS; I'd bet anything amputation hurts more.

Can't tell if this is just a headache, or if my brain is about to pop.

I know I said earlier that amputation hurts more, but losing a championship probably hurts the most.

No pain no gain? I'll take the loss.

Not sure if this headache is sinuses, caffeine, stress, or dehydration. Most likely it's some kind of unholy combination of all of the above.

Everyone's tough until you stub your toe.

Summer Thoughts

Lovely day, might go for a walk. Unless it's too hot… or too cold… there's a real sweet spot that I operate in.

My favorite thing about a hot day is when just walking up the stairs makes me sweat all over my body. It's like a free little shower.

I love the fact that the weather is great when I'm stuck at work, and usually terrible when it's my day off.

Fill me with your delicious energy, Sky Daddy.

Sunscreen is for losers!

If I set up by the water, I'll have to move when the tide comes back in, but if I set up away from the water, it'll be a much further walk to the water. Furthermore, I can't set up near people because people suck, but I don't want to walk too far from the entrances…

Another thing is, I can't be in a spot too good because then people will set up next to me, and again, people suck. I guess I'll set up away from the water and away from most people and take a nap so that the water won't be too far when I wake up…nap time…aaaand the tide was actually going out, so now I have to walk a mile to get to the water.

Where are these so-called boys?
Probably all over Manhattan.

Small waves today; if I sit down, it'll feel like I'm at one of those cool beaches with big waves.

I am the red lobster.

"I think the smell of rain is overrated. You could achieve the same thing by throwing a bucket of water into the air and taking a deep breath through your nose.

I hate sunshowers; it's like, pick a lane.

I guess I just really don't understand the love of rainy days; honestly, they kinda piss me off. Even if my plans only involved staying inside, and the rain technically didn't ruin anything, it still feels like it did.

People love the rain. I, personally, hate the rain. But no matter your feelings on the rain, most people can't help but say,
"We needed it."

Winter Thoughts

I love waking up on a sunny winter's day, throwing the curtains open, and being blinded by the glare of the sun reflecting off the snow, as it burns out my eyes with the intensity of a new galaxy being born.

The first snowfall and the last one elicit similar emotional responses but on the opposite end of the spectrum.

I was home-schooled, so I have no idea what a snow day is like. Sounds nice though.

Sledding is great fun, but then you have to trek back up a giant hill. I think this is why adults don't really go sledding.

Yeah, snow is so beautiful. It covers the ground with shining water crystals, creating a wonderful atmosphere of joy. Until you have to go out and shovel for three hours.

We like to think of fireplaces as warm and cozy. A nice aesthetic to our winter evenings, but fire used to be the only way we'd literally not die on that so-called "cozy" evening.

Winter is great in December, but after that it, just feels like an oppressive force trying to beat you into submission.

Skiing is really just an excuse to sit in a lodge and day drink.

The Silent Judgments

You Keep in Your Head

I'm not saying you can't pull socks all the way up your shins, but I am saying you shouldn't.

Oh, that's the music you're gonna play? Good to know you have trash taste.

Stop talking like you're some kind of gangster; you're from rural Maine.

More things in the world would get done if people weren't so long-winded.

Oh wow, you're gonna be a little late?

Color me shocked.

I know the only reason you're singing ahead of the song is so we hear you and say, "Oh wow, you're sooooo good! Why aren't you doing this professionally?"

No Chloe, I think a gallon and a half of perfume is the perfect amount.

Sunglasses inside is a bold choice.

Quick coughing like your lungs are about to jump out of your throat. I know you just want attention and sympathy.

Oh cool, a "Coexist" bumper sticker
…did you wanna tell me about Mars being in retrograde and where I can find the best pinot grigio?

I think when you turn sixty, haddock becomes your favorite thing in the whole world. All you ever want to order is haddock. At Fifty-nine, you're kinda warm on haddock, by sixty, it's all you ever want to eat 'til the day you die. Just order something else for once.

Oh, you're tired because you spent all night drinking and playing video games, knowing full well you needed to be at work in the morning? I'm supposed to have sympathy because...?

Oh God, is that what I really look like?

Thinking About Your Family

Whenever I'm away from my family, I miss them, especially over an extended period of time. Then, we all hang out and I miss being away from my family.

I don't even like group chats, I like my family just enough to reluctantly be a part of it.

Does anyone actually enjoy family reunions?

Family is so weird; they make you deal with unexpected situations all the time, and you have no choice in the matter because they're family. I swear, this is the last time I'll help my grandmother defraud the government and bury a body.

Sometimes, I sit and wonder how many things I actually got away with as a kid. Or is it just the things I thought I was getting away with? Like, did my parents know I never snuck out and was always in bed by 9:00? Or do they wish to believe their son was actually cool?

Your cousins: the real life equivalent of a character randomizer.

They say friends are the family you choose, but if you adopt…
you can also choose your family.

My siblings, the people I am most likely to kill for, and be the one to kill them.

They say blood is thicker than water,
and like, obviously.

My parents always ask how I turned out so snarky, I
tell them to ask the people who raised me.

Oh, you don't want to go to the retirement home? Well, I wanted the new Xbox as a kid.

I'm Not Drunk, You're Drunk

I know claw machines are rigged, I know that every time I put in a dollar, I'd be better off tossing it on the sidewalk and walking away. But because I won one once as a ten-year-old, I am convinced I can win it every single time. Just one more game - I know I'll win this $2 prize if I just spend twenty-five more dollars.

I think a good name for an 80s cover band would be "Newy Lewis and the Hues."

I was self-educated, and

I learned from the best.

I really love these guys. Better express it by constantly making fun of them and questioning every decision they ever make.

You ever wonder what it would be like if spontaneous human combustion was actually a thing? Like you're hanging out with Darryl and bam! You just freaking explode.
That'd be rough.

At this point,
this is a conversation without a point.

I'm having fun, but this is the last time I ever want to do one of these teenage-style sleepovers... Oh god, am I old now?

Just don't be the drunkest guy in the room.

The alcohol has unlocked my ability to literally be the greatest at anything and everything.

Bush = Toilet

Anything can be considered a bed,
when you think about it.

Every fart is a shart, since every time you fart, microscopic amounts of poo come out.

What do you mean it's only 8:30?

I totally made it across the room
walking in a straight line.

I should totally do parkour across this dumpster.

Party Thoughts

I always get weary when the party starts at nine p.m.

Pool party?
Ehhh.
Hot tub party?
Heck yeah!

If truth or dare comes out at an adult party, it's time to leave.

Booze is not food, if you're throwing a party, please feed your guests.

Have I been talking to this person for five minutes,
or five hours?

Italian Plumber Kart is coming out? Hopefully
everybody is ready to not be my friend anymore.

The chips are gone...
my night just got a little worse.

I don't know any of these people. I'd better go stand in the corner, and try not to be seen.

What's that? Through the murmur of the crowd,
I hear mention of a topic I, too, am interested in.
I must snake my way through groups of people to
interject with my fun facts.

Parties generally make me question my friends'
musical taste.

It's so great to catch up with everyone.
I am having a wonderful time. Oh no…
here comes the conversation killer.

I'mma just dance out of this conversation.

Why do we go over to the same house to party? No matter what, or who, the party is for? How is the party house even determined? And why are the owners of the dedicated party house so weird whenever someone brings up the idea of throwing a party at someone else's house?

If one of the bedrooms isn't filled to the brim with coats, is it even a real party?

Thoughts You Have the Next Morning

The only thing I desire in this moment is the greasiest fast-food breakfast sandwich I can find.

I'm scared to check my phone…

I spent how much?

There is no shame in this walk.

I'm proud of what I accomplished last night.

Nobody told me your 20s
end before you actually turn 30.

I think I need to have a
serious chat with myself.

I hope I didn't end any friendships
through my powers of debate.

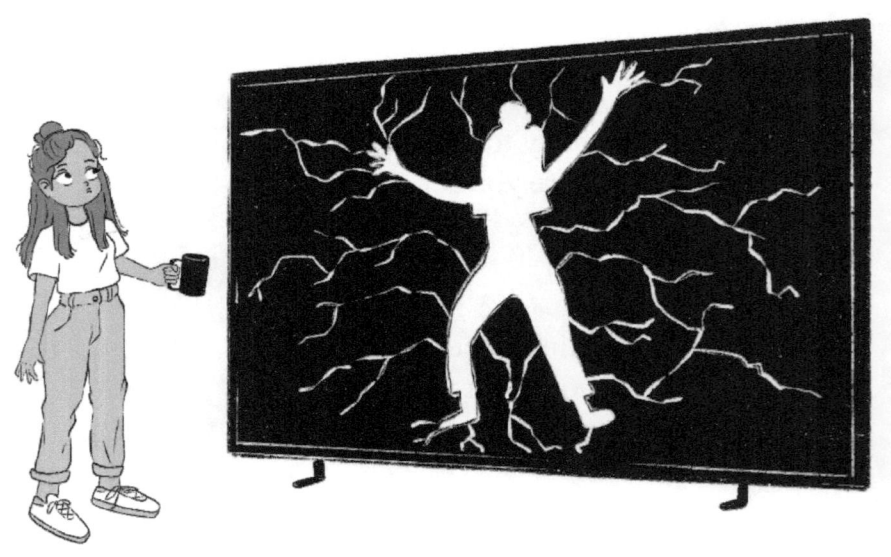

There's no way I actually fell into a TV last night.

In retrospect, mixing all the alcohol like a fast-food soda machine is a bad idea.
At least I wasn't the drunkest guy in the room…or was I?

How did the couch feel so comfortable last night, but feel like the sidewalk this morning?
Whose couch is this anyway?

Next time I'll remember to drink water.

I've gotta keep in mind I can't actually sing as well as I think I can.

What if, while I'm on the bus, the semi driving next to us right now slams into the side of the bus, sending the bus and everyone inside over the bridge, and into the dark depths of the river below? I'd have mere seconds to react while we fly through the air. If my timing is right, I can grab onto the seat in front of me and hold on, hopefully that minimizes the impact on my body. Then, I'll need to break open the window and swim as hard as I can. Should I try and bring my backpack? It has all my things in it, I'll need my things. Should I try to swim up with other passengers? I've heard that saving people from drowning is the best way to find yourself being drowned. I'll need to get to the surface fast enough to call 911, then I'll go back for passengers…oh, the truck passed us fifteen minutes ago.

What if, while I'm lying in bed, a car crashes into the side of my house, knocking out a whole wall? Assuming the whole structure doesn't buckle, I'll need to run down and make sure the cats are safe and can't run out. I guess as a human, I should check on the driver first, but I'm definitely going to check on the cats first. Assuming the driver is okay and doesn't need medical attention, I'll probably just start unloading into this guy. I mean, who drives into a house? They're probably drunk, but still! It's a lot easier to not drive into the house than it is to actually hit the house. I should probably call the cops next, and then my boss to explain why I can't come into work today. Actually, come to think of it, I'll probably have a fat insurance settlement, so, I'll probably just quit on the spot. God, where would I stay? I don't wanna stay in a house with a car-sized hole in it. That would let hella bugs in, and I do not like the idea of hella bugs. Oh man, imagine if this happened in the winter, there would be no way to heat the house. This would be quite the pickle I'd find myself in.

What happens if I go downstairs in the middle of the night and there are several armed thugs in my house? Why are they here? If they're here to rob me, then I might just let them carry on. But what if they're actually here to kill me? Why are they here to kill me? Maybe because when I went to the coffee shop, a secret government agent slipped a thumb drive into my pocket and these are actually Russian mercenaries here because they think I work for the CIA. I don't want to be killed due to a misunderstanding, but I can't let Russia have state secrets either. I'll have no choice but to fight them off. I'll grab the fire poker and hurl it through the air like a javelin. Then, I'll throw my entire body sideways, into them. Then it's simply a matter of one-on-one combat with the rest of them. That's exactly what I'll do.

What if, while walking to work one day, I find a wallet with $20,000 in it? The right thing to do would be to turn it in and hope it finds its owner, but what if I just did the wrong thing? I mean, everyone tries to do the right thing, we all hope, given the chance we'd drive in quickly and take the bullet, but what if I just kept it? Who would know? More importantly, how would they know? I could very easily just spend it in small amounts so as to not attract attention. It would be dumb to spend it all at once. That'll definitely put a target on my back - probably a federal target. Guess I'll just toss a coin to find out if I'm going to be good or not... Great, now I'm a legit supervillain.

Maybe I'm an alien. Perhaps I was sent here as a goodwill ambassador for the people of Earth, and when I hit a certain age, all of that information will be unlocked. It would make sense to have me be a sleeper agent. This way, I'm fully immersed in the culture. I'll know what to say to both sides. I'll have ties to two races. I could single-handedly bring about a new golden age. I won't, since most of these people suck and don't deserve a golden age. I'll just inform the high council of Thebulas III to leave these people alone and let them continue to wallow in self-misery until they grow up a little. Wow, who knew I would be so harsh? Some goodwill ambassador I turned out to be.

What if the Earth really had been flat and all of those ancient explorers had fallen off the globe? We would have no way of ever knowing because there would have been no way for them to tell us. What would have happened? We would have just kept sending out ship after ship, each of them falling to their doom. "Well, this is the direction Columbus was heading; I estimate this is about as far as he could have gotten. But where could he…OH MY GOD, SHIP OVERBOARD!" How many people would we have just sent out to find them, and then to go find the finders?

I know the CIA can hear my thoughts.

I'm always nice to AI,
just in case they end up taking over.

I'm pretty sure this is all a simulation; how else
can you explain the moon being cheese?
That wouldn't even make sense in real life.

People who wear tin foil hats are stupid, you have to use lead. Tin foil is a signal booster... duh!

I can feel the silent judgment of birds.

I played a Beatles album backwards, and I heard Paul say, "You're a moron and you're going to ruin your record by playing it backwards."
This definitely means he's dead.

We always thought we were watching TV, but it was the TV watching us all along.

If a bear $%!#$ in the woods, does it make a sound?

What if toys really are alive?

I know the CIA is honing in on me because of the information that they don't want us to know about, that I found while doing my independent research online.

Chores and All the Thoughts That Come with Them

Why should I bother cleaning the back windows as well as the front ones? Nobody should be back here looking through my windows, and if they are, how clean the windows are will be the least of my concerns.

Didn't I do this last week?
Ugh, and I'll be doing it again next week?

I don't condone the idea of servitude, but I do get it.

I keep gaslighting myself into thinking the washing machine is just about to finish so I shouldn't walk away... I've been standing here for twenty-five minutes.

The sink looks so good after doing the dishes, but I know I'm going to go into another room and find a coffee cup someone left lying around. I'm not going to bother going through all the effort for one cup, but my nice sink is going to look so pedestrian with one single coffee-stained cup staring back at me.

I really need to update my productivity playlist. Can't work if the vibes are wrong.

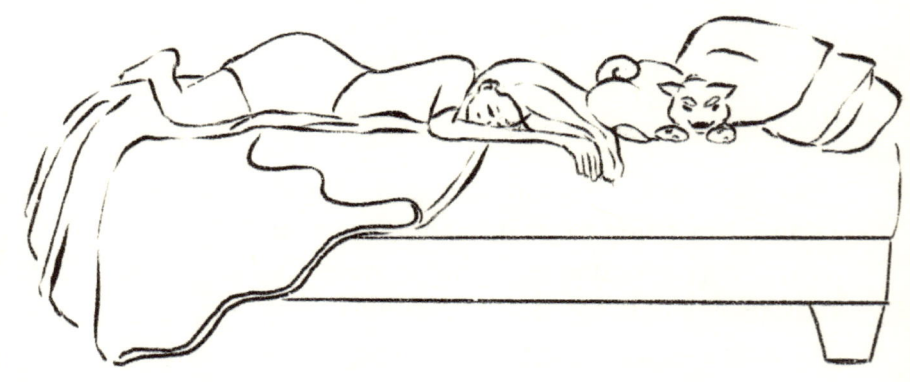

I should, and could, be doing something,
but I shan't.

Do you ever find yourself looking out into the distance, waiting for a productive thought to come to your head, but then you realize no thoughts have come to your head at all? That's what I was just doing.

Cleaning up this room would take fifteen minutes, but I'm not going to do it for three weeks and trick my brain into thinking it's worse than it really is.

Those dishes won't do themselves, but maybe God will perform a little miracle for me.

Problems just go away on their own, right?

"Don't ask me to do anything, I'm feeling weird today!"

I know it's only late July but it's gonna snow in five months and cover up the lawn, so why do I really need to mow?

I've done five minutes, time to reward myself with a three-hour nap.

Wow, that fifteen-minute chore only took forty-five minutes.

Ugh, it's like some kinda slob lives here.

Daytime TV and What It Does to Your Brain

I wish I were the next contestant on

"The Price is Right."

I really feel like at this point, soap operas could afford some better cameras.

Why do they keep bringing up type 2 diabetes?

That sure is a lot of side effects.

This game show host also has a talk show?

I didn't know a talk show
could have so much yelling.

Oh, he is definitely the father, pshhh, scumbag.

That's right! You tell him, Judy!

This has got to be a fake product.

The longer I watch this, the more I can feel my brain literally turning into sludge that will begin dripping out of my ear any second.

Money Thoughts

I could have afforded to pay all my bills this month if only I hadn't spent my youth buying candy bars, but how was I supposed to know about inflation as an eight-year-old?

They say "more money, more problems," but it seems like the people with more money have fewer problems, Perhaps I only think that because I'm capable of critical thinking.

I feel like I've actually managed to save up a little bit. This can only mean that something is about to happen for I'll need to dip into my savings for.

I'd have a lot more money if I didn't have such expensive hobbies.

I think we should get rid of cash, not because it's outdated or less convenient, but because it's disgusting. Just think about how many hands and other various body parts have come in contact with that cash. You really want me to carry around wads of biohazard just so I can purchase something?
No, sir.

I want to save up money to be able to retire someday and not have to worry so much. My wife wants to save money so our pets can live in the lap of luxury.

Whenever I watch an old movie, I use an inflation calculator to see if the actors are being compensated fairly.

Well, I should have about $250 dollars left in my account. Lemme just double check it real quick... $26.89

How am I supposed to stay in the positive with all these gosh dang bank fees?

I'm really gonna have to have a serious chat with whoever is in charge of my checking account.

Traveling Thoughts

I'm pretty sure I didn't forget anything,
but I always say that only to end up realizing that
I did once I get to my destination.

Whoever decided that we didn't need airflow on a
bus, should be arrested.

I wish I had more comfortable shoes. Of course,
I don't want to pay for more comfortable shoes.

I really don't want to be late. I need to be at my gate no less than two hours before departure.

It's amazing how different the quality of a fast-food restaurant can change from city to city.

God, I hope that ungodly stench isn't coming from me.

After a few days of straight travel, I don't think it would be the worst thing if the plane crashed with me still inside.

Why does the toilet in the bus smell so unearthly? There is nothing else on the planet that smells like the 2' x 2' bathroom on the bus. The second that chemical concoction penetrates my nostrils, I'm instantly transported back to every single time I've ridden the bus. That stuff is definitely connected to the Illuminati.

There should be a chill bus that's just recliners. Not bus seat recliners, but the real deal. Straight-up furniture, bolted to the ground. That would make this twelve-hour ride so much nicer.

Road trips are fun in theory. I don't care how close you are with someone. A few days on the road together and you will have contemplated murder at least nine times.

Better check to make sure I still have my wallet another twenty-three times.

Do I wake up the perfect stranger who fell asleep on my shoulder, or just let them be?

Thoughts You Have on Vacation.

I wonder how much it would cost to move here?

More hotels would have my money if they didn't tack on "service," "cleaning," or "resort" fees. Just have that included in the price. I'm not going to give my money to someone who is trying to deceive me.

My ideal vacation is actually just staying home and enjoying the quiet.

When I'm on vacation, I'm so hard to get a hold of, I may as well be dead.

If AirBnB has a cleaning fee, why do I need to pull the linens off the bed, wipe out the sink, vacuum the floor, leave nothing in the dishwasher, and take out all the trash? What cleaning are you charging for? I've done everything.

If you bring work with you, it's not really a vacation. So, don't be surprised if your family starts to resent you.

Theme parks, a vacation from the quiet.

OOOO, meat on a stick, don't mind if I do.

I make sure to have a buffer day after vacation, because doing a whole day of travel just to get home, erases any and all relaxation my body was holding on to.

There are a million things I want to do! If I'm lucky I'll get to do three of them.

Sometimes, after a vacation
I need a vacation vacation.

$25 for a T-shirt that says, "Vacation Boy"
Sign me up!

Thoughts You Have While

Enjoying A Dining Establishment

If you're going to leave a pitcher of water on the table, why does it only fill a glass and a half of water?

I want to order an appetizer, but I don't know if I'm
actually hungry enough…
and I won't know until after I eat it.

Every time you order a steak, it really does feel like
rolling the dice if they actually know how to temp a
steak back there.

I love coming here.
Sometimes all you want is to be treated like a king
and that's me, the King of IHOP.

Ooo, bread sticks!

My food wasn't great the last seventeen times
I ate here, but it's certainly
the most conveniently located.

Our server is so friendly, but I know
she's dead inside.

I know any food coming out of here fifteen
minutes before closing time was not made with love.

Carpet in a restaurant is a ballsy move.

If you're "eating good" in the collection of houses you live near, here is how you make the perfect mixed drink.

78% ice

10% non-alcoholic mixer

10 % more ice

1% garnish

5% "love"

5% alcohol.

Whenever I hear a table complain and make weird vague threats to the staff, I know that 98% of the time, it's a problem the customer created. But you gotta commend their commitment to being a liar.

When you get the bill,
there are only two reactions.
"Hey, that's really not that bad."
Or
"How on earth is it that much?
Why does a soda refill cost $3?"

You will not tempt me with dessert!
Well…
couldn't hurt to look.

Thoughts You Have When You're Trying to Fall Asleep, But Your Brain Decides It Won't Let You

If I fall asleep right now,
I'll get seven hours of sleep.

Do my animals know how much I love them?

Was there a real bubble boy?
And what happened to him?

Jesus Christ, what is that?
Oh, haha, it's my blanket.
I thought it was a scary face.

If I fall asleep now, I'll get six hours and fifteen minutes of sleep.

Did that barista get my name wrong on purpose?

What is my weight in gold?

If I fall asleep now,
I'll get five hours and
twenty-five minutes of sleep.

Did I leave the hallway light on?
I don't think so... I should check...
but I really don't want to.

I really should have remembered
I already had mayo.

I wonder if I can still climb a tree?

What was that?
Old house noise?
Animal?
Ghost?
An animal chasing a ghost in my old house?

How much force would actually be required to get a cow over the moon?

If I fall asleep now,
I'll get three hours of sleep.
Is there any point in trying anymore?

Was that person flirting with me fifteen years ago? Now that I think about it, I think they were. Who knows how my life could have turned out?

I'm thirsty, my cup has no water, and if I get out of bed, I'm gonna have to start the whole "falling asleep" process all over again, but if I don't get water, it's gonna keep me up even longer.

Must resist urge to use phone.

Resisting urge to use phone, failed.

www.ingramcontent.com/pod-product-compliance
Lightning Source LLC
Chambersburg PA
CBHW060352080526
44583CB00012B/281